I can draw!

Dinosaurs, Dragons
& Prehistoric Creatures

Walter Foster

Jr.

I can draw!

Dinosaurs, Dragons
& Prehistoric Creatures

**Learn to draw reptilian beasts
and fantasy characters step by step!**

www.walterfoster.com
3 Wrigley, Suite A
Irvine, CA 92618

Artwork © Fleurus Editions, Paris-2014
Published by Walter Foster Jr.,
an imprint of Quarto Publishing Group USA Inc.
Illustrated by Philippe Legendre
Written by Janessa Osle

3 5 7 9 10 8 6 4

Table of Contents

Tools & Materials

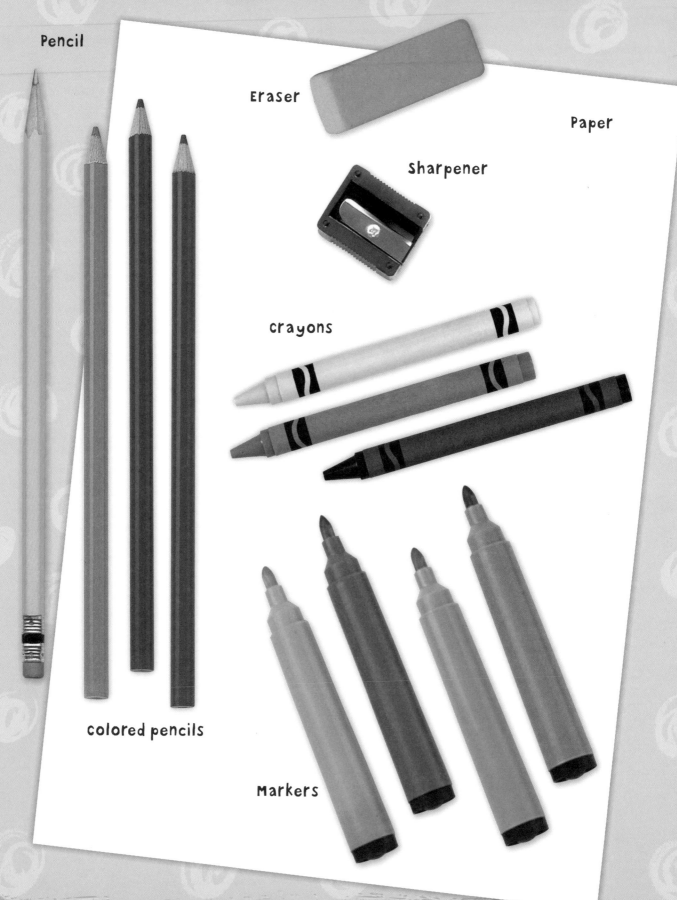

Pencil

Eraser

Paper

Sharpener

crayons

colored pencils

Markers

The Color Wheel

The color wheel shows the relationships between colors. It helps us understand how the different colors relate to and react with one another. It's easy to make your own color wheel!

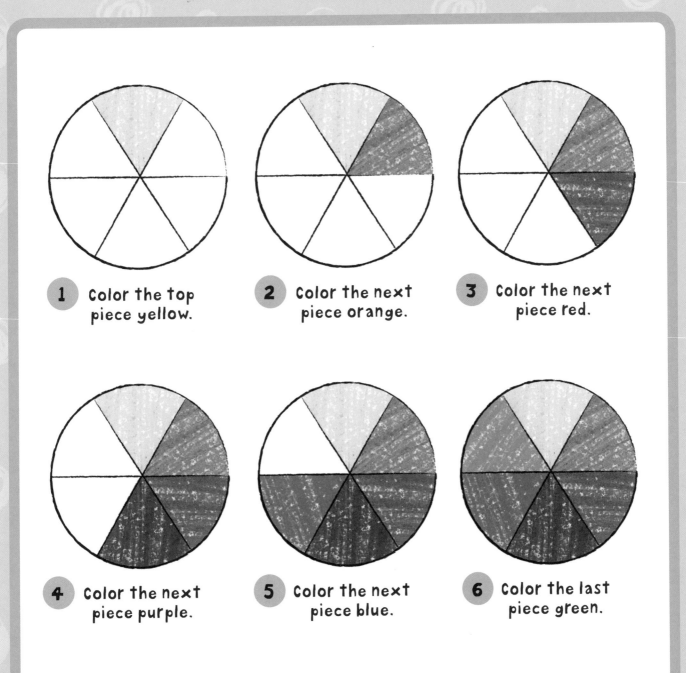

1 Color the top piece yellow.

2 Color the next piece orange.

3 Color the next piece red.

4 Color the next piece purple.

5 Color the next piece blue.

6 Color the last piece green.

Getting Started

Warm up your hand by drawing some squiggles and shapes on a piece of scrap paper.

Draw a square

Draw an oval

Draw a circle

Draw a rectangle

Draw a triangle

If you can draw a few basic shapes, you can draw just about anything!

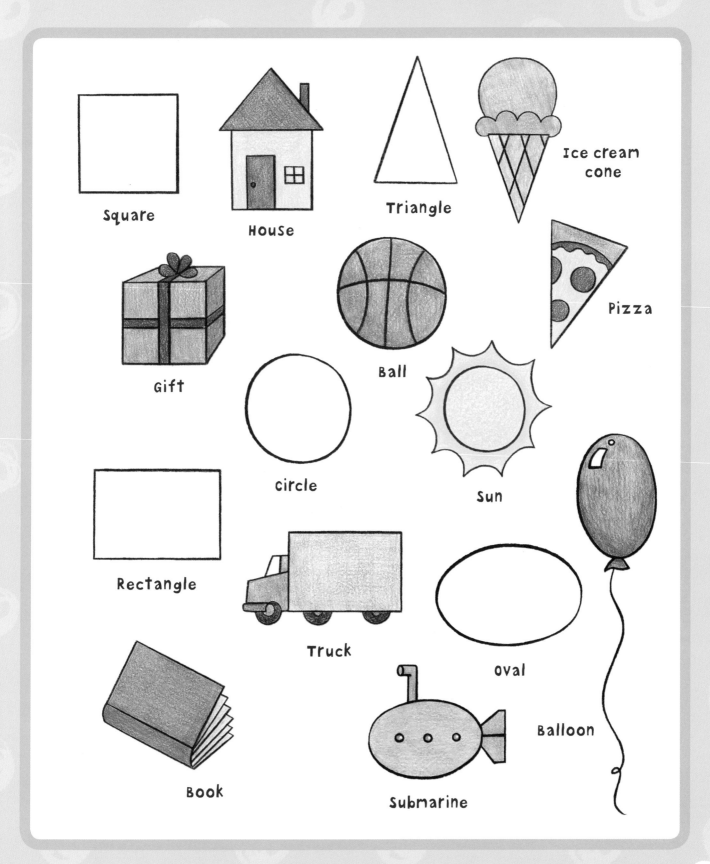

Square

House

Triangle

Ice cream cone

Gift

Ball

Pizza

circle

Sun

Rectangle

Truck

Oval

Book

Submarine

Balloon

Iguanodon

The Iguanodon was very large and spent most of its time grazing on all four legs, even though it was able to walk on two!

Mammoth

The mammoth, a relative of today's elephant, lived during the last ice age.

Dimetrodon

This carnivore grew to more than 11½ feet long and had a large sail on its back to help regulate its temperature.

Saber-toothed Cat

This cat-like carnivore was named for the pair of long, sharp teeth in its upper jaw!

Diplodocus

The Diplodocus was the longest dinosaur that lived during the Late Jurassic Period!

Triceratops

This dinosaur is known for the frill of bone at the back of its skull and the three prominent horns on its head!

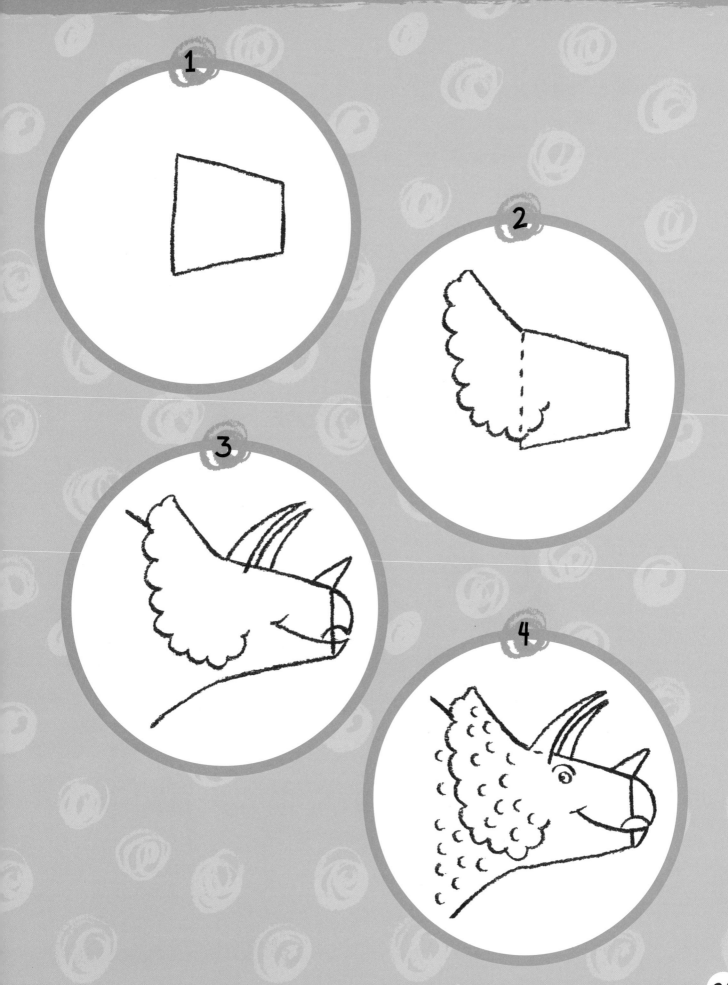

Woolly Rhinoceros

This hairy species of rhinoceros became extinct at the end of the last ice age.

Pteranodon

This flying reptile from the Late Cretaceous Period had powerful wings and a long beak for catching fish in the ocean.

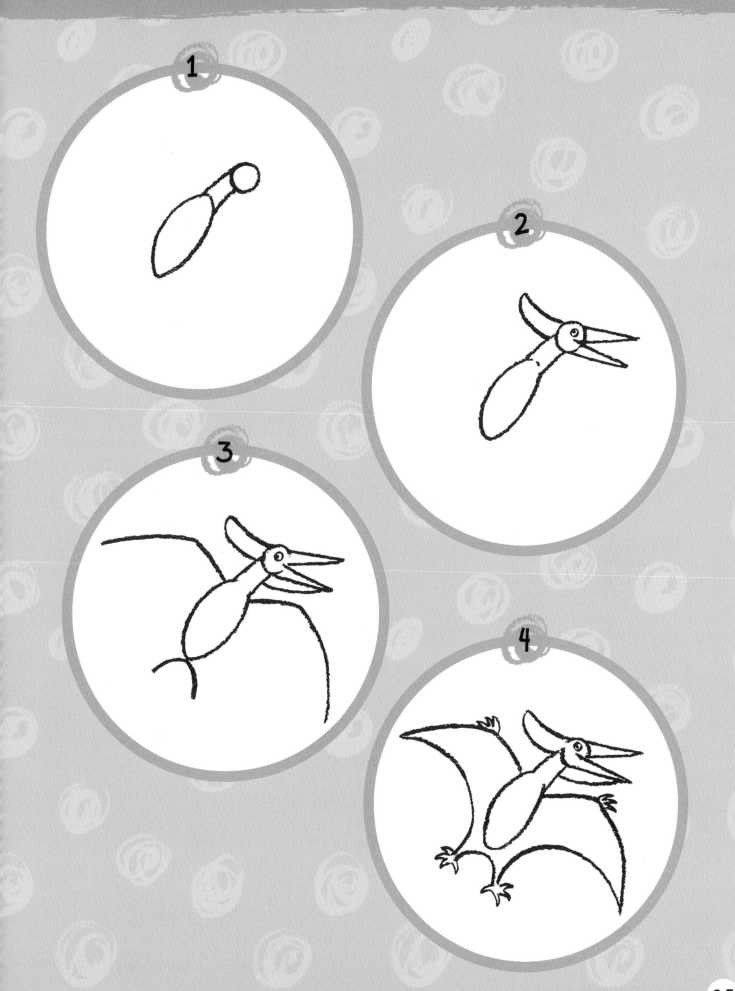

Auroch

The auroch was a wild ox that lived in central Poland; it has been found in many cave paintings!

Tyrannosaurus Rex

This large predator lived from the Late Jurassic Period to the Cretaceous Period and walked on its powerful hind limbs!

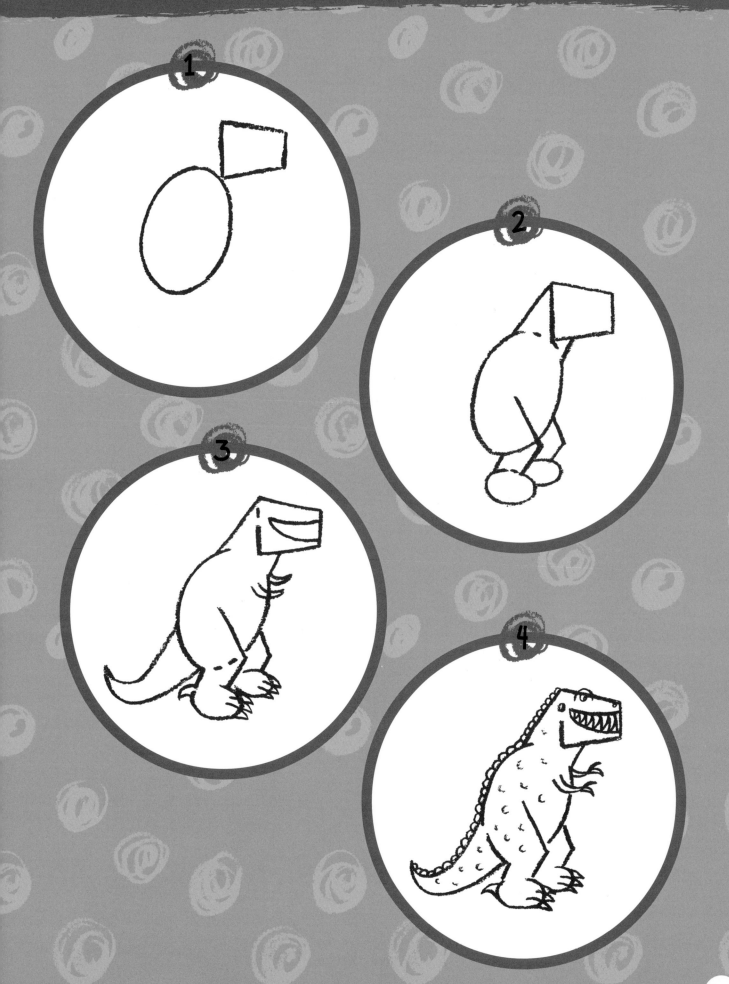

Dragon

Dragons are legendary creatures from myths and fairy tales.

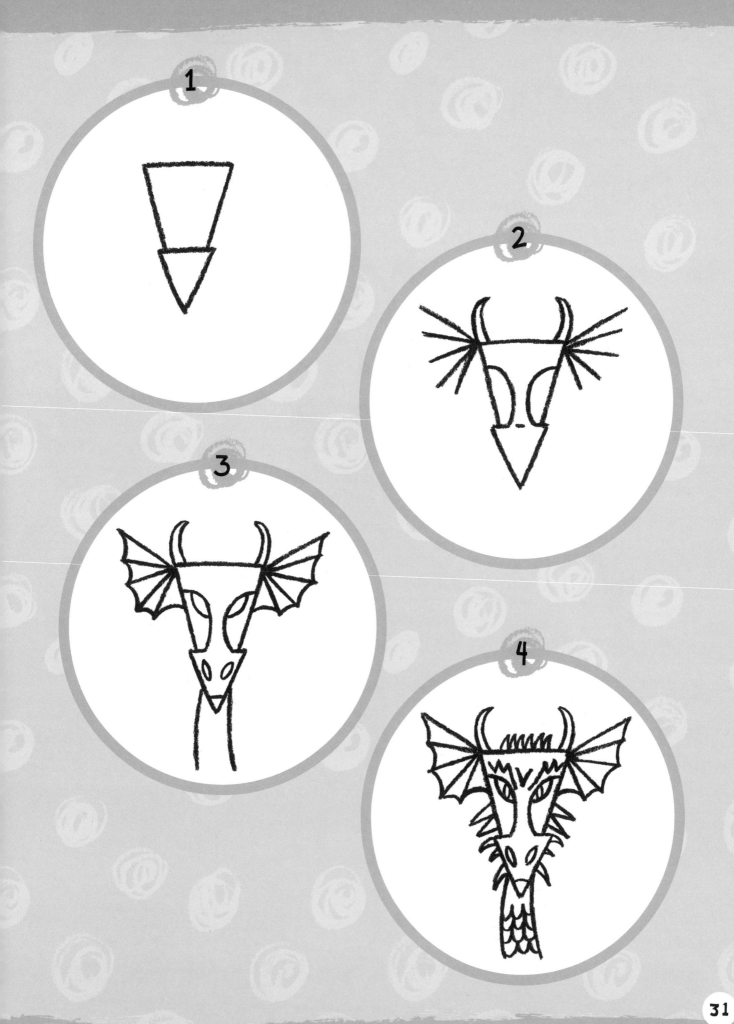

cro-Magnon

cro-Magnons were prehistoric humans with strong and powerful bodies built for hunting!

Pterodactyl

Pterodactyls were flying lizards with pointed wings, short legs, and long beaks with lots of teeth.

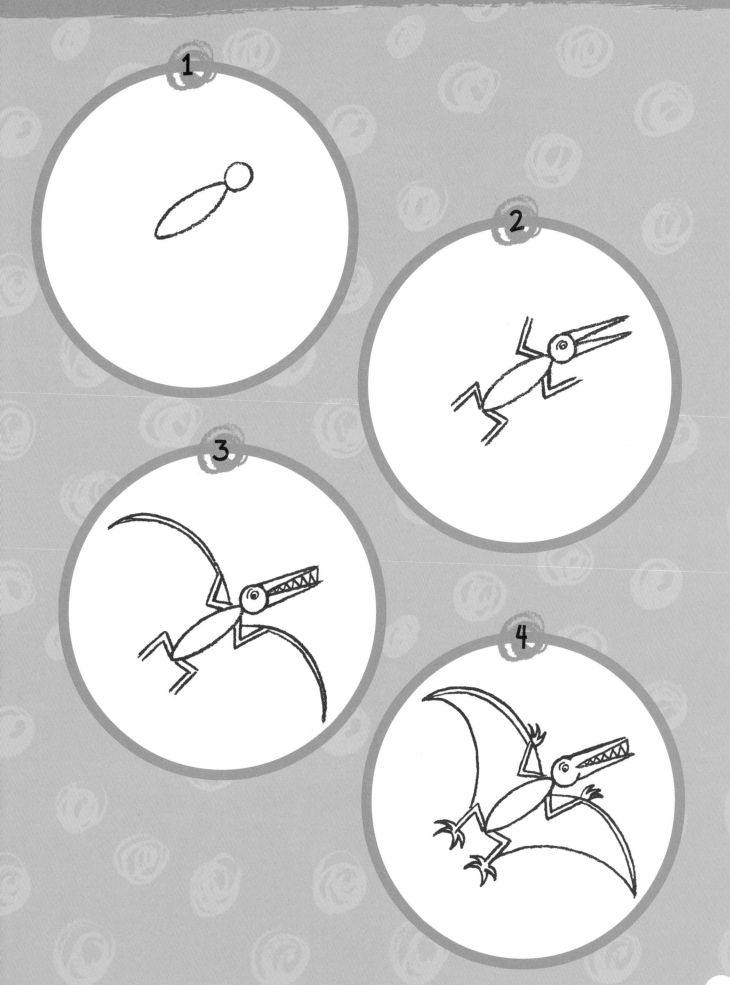

Water Dragon

This mythical dragon is said to live in large bodies of water, such as rivers, lakes, and the sea.

Ankylosaurus

This plant-eating dinosaur was covered in bony spikes, and its tail ended in a large, bony club!

Horse Cave Painting

The first cave paintings by early humans date back to the Late Stone Age, almost 50,000 years ago!

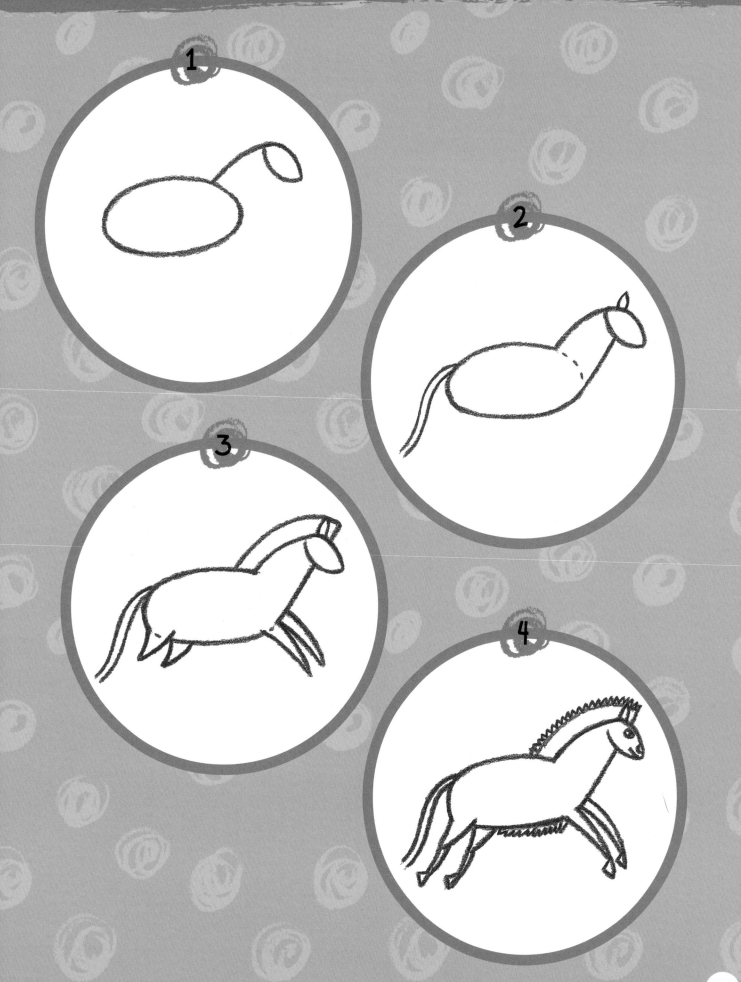

41

Chinese Dragon

In Chinese folklore, the dragon is a symbol of power and good luck!

stegosaurus

This dinosaur is known for its spiked tail and the large triangular bony plates along its back!

Fire Dragon

This powerful dragon can breathe fire and has a very short temper!

The End